Civil War Soldier Life: In Camp & Battle

By George F. Williams

Introduction & New Material
By Patrick A. Schroeder

SCHROEDER PUBLICATIONS
2014

Cover: An early war photograph of Civil War soldiers in camp. *(Collection of Patrick A. Schroeder)*

Cover Design: Maria Dorsett Schroeder

Published by
SCHROEDER PUBLICATIONS
131 Tanglewood Drive
Lynchburg, VA 24502
www.civilwar-books.com
civilwarbooks@yahoo.com

Printed by
Farmville Printing
Farmville, Virginia

ISBN-1-889246-04-2

INTRODUCTION

If I ever had one wish that could be granted, it would be to talk with an actual Civil War soldier. Unless time travel ever becomes reality, it is impossible. Have you ever wanted to talk to a Civil War soldier? This book by George Williams answers the questions most people would ask a Civil War soldier if they could. Williams would be an ideal candidate to respond. He served for the first three years of the war as a soldier and the last year as a journalist. He tells about going into battle for the first time and how it felt later as a veteran. Williams explains the difficulties for Americans making the transition from civilian to soldier. He writes of the pleasures of camp life, about winter quarters, and gives insight on the generals and their nicknames. Williams peppers the material with first-hand accounts and humorous incidents. The main idea behind writing the articles was to educate people who had not seen military service in the war. Williams hoped to share the feelings and memories retained by the veterans and to help explain why they recalled the war so poignantly.

The old standard on Civil War soldier life, primarily from the Federal perspective, is *Hardtack & Coffee: The Unwritten Story of Army Life* by John D. Billings, who served with the 10th Massachusetts Light Artillery. Billings gave detailed information of countless aspects of army life, and for a serious historian, it is indispensable. However, no matter how interested one is, parts of the book drag with minute details. This is not the case with Williams' writing. He covers the various aspects of soldier life with incidents and intrigue that leads the reader to the next section. In short, these articles are eminently readable--a miniature *Hardtack & Coffee.*

Williams' articles are even more impressive because he is unbiased and pays respect to the soldiers both North and South. In 1884, his book, *Bullet and Shell: The Civil War as a Soldier Saw It,* was published and remains a classic today. In October 1884, he penned "Lights and Shadows of Army Life" for *The Century Magazine.* The other piece, "Crossing the Lines," he wrote for *Blue and Gray; The Patriotic American Magazine,* in 1893. This piece gives his account of the Battle of the Wilderness, his wounding and capture, and his interview with Confederate General Robert E. Lee. Both articles were

3

illustrated by the talented wartime artist Edwin Forbes.

The assembling of this work is intended to fill the void of a small, readable, reliable and affordable account of Civil War soldier life. There are accounts of Lincoln, Lee and McClellan, not contained in biographies of those men. This book includes a biographical sketch of Williams to familiarize the reader with the author's background and experiences. *Civil War Soldier Life: In Camp and Battle* is enjoyable reading and invaluable for an understanding of the soldiers who participated in our country's most devastating conflict.

Patrick A. Schroeder

(Donald Wisnoski Collection)

George F. Williams
Circa 1863

4

George Forrester Williams

Soldiers of the American Civil War were, in general, literate and expressive. Their letters, diaries and memoirs have been treasured for generations. However, George Williams had an advantage over the typical enlisted man in that he had worked as a newspaper reporter prior to the conflict. He survived battles and wounds, and in a long and colorful postwar career, penned a spirited semi-autobiographical novel- - *Bullet and Shell*. He also wrote several shorter pieces that drew from his wartime experiences with the 5th and 146th New York Volunteers.

Williams' father charged with the Scots Grays at Waterloo. George was born March 21, 1837, on the Rock of Gibraltar, where his father's regiment was stationed. As a child, George saw much of the world and lived for a time in the East and West Indies and the Gold Coast of Africa. The Williams family ended its travels in Canada. While there, his parents died. At age 13, the orphan arrived in the United States with only three dollars in his pocket and took up the printing trade. For several years he set type for the *New York Times*. One evening a fire occurred in the city after the editor went home. Williams did a write up of the story and got an early morning extra in circulation. This caught the attention of the chief editor, Henry J. Raymond, who then made him part of the reportorial and editorial staff. Williams began to make a name for himself. He was covering the events of the Virginia Secession Convention in the spring of 1861, when the state voted to leave the Union. Fearing for his life, Williams fled Richmond without retrieving his trunk from the Spottswood Hotel.

On July 21, 1861, Williams enlisted in the 5th New York Volunteer Infantry. Colonel Abram Duryée had organized this unit and outfitted the men in colorful uniforms patterned after those of the famous French Zouaves. With a red fez for a head piece, a short blue jacket trimmed in red, a long red sash trimmed in light blue, baggy red pantaloons, and white leggings, it was a splendid uniform. By the time Williams joined Duryée's Zouaves, the regiment had already fought in the first battle of the Civil War at Big Bethel on June 10, 1861, and were dubbed "red-legged devils" by their Southern foes.

At the time of his enlistment, Williams was 24 years old, stood 6'1", had auburn hair and gray eyes. Upon arriving at Fortress Monroe on the Virginia peninsula, he was assigned to Company B of the unit.

By that fall, the Zouaves were stationed in Baltimore where, throughout the winter, the 5th trained to proficiency in tactics, skirmish drill and the bayonet exercise. On January 9, 1862, Williams was promoted corporal, and in the spring of 1862, he accompanied the 5th New York as the Army of the Potomac began its campaign against Richmond. During the siege of Yorktown, Williams, like many other soldiers, took sick with fever. Typhoid fever incapacitated him from May 9 to 18, when he recovered enough to take charge of the guard on the Sanitary Commission steamer *Elm City* at White House Landing. Corporal Williams longed to rejoin the regiment, and in late June, encountered Colonel Gouverneur K. Warren, commander of the brigade, and returned to the unit with him. Williams made it back to the red-legs just in time to participate in the Battle of Gaines' Mill on June 27, 1862. Again, the red-legs won the admiration of friend and foe alike when they launched a ferocious counter charge against the Confederate onslaught. A third of the regiment was killed or wounded in the engagement, and Williams sustained a wound in the right foot.

As the Army of the Potomac withdrew, Williams limped along with his regiment. After reaching the James River, he "hobbled" over to the landing and found Dr. Gibbs who was a surgeon aboard the *Elm City*. Gibbs operated on the wound, then ordered Williams to a berth. Williams began his convalescence in Baltimore, then received a furlough home. Upon recovery, he reported to Major Harmon Hull who was in charge of recruiting for the 5th in New York. Fortunately for Williams, he was assigned to assist in that duty from July 23 through January 1863 while the regiment suffered enormous casualties at the Battle of Second Manassas. The red-legs lost 297 men--124 of them killed or mortally wounded. This was the highest number of Federal infantry regimental fatalities during a single battle for the war.

Williams rejoined the regiment in February 1863 and in March, he was detailed as company clerk. Following the Battle of Chancellorsville, on May 4, 1863, the men who enlisted at the outset of the war for a two-year term of service departed for home. Williams and 236 other three-year enlistees were transferred to the 146th New York Infantry to complete their unexpired terms of service. Williams was assigned to Company G, but in June was transferred to Company B. That month the 146th New York adopted a Zouave uniform of their own, quite different from the 5th New York--a light blue Zouave uniform with a red sash, both trimmed with yellow.

On July 2, 1863, Williams and the 146th helped defend the slopes of Little Round Top at Gettysburg. Later that year he was promoted sergeant. On January 15, 1864, he joined the regimental field and staff as principal musician. Perhaps because of his stature, Williams was appointed color sergeant in April. On May 5, 1864, he grasped the regimental colors as the unit charged across Saunders' Field at the Battle of the Wilderness. As the Zouaves advanced, Williams was struck by three bullets in the first Confederate volley, wounding him in both hips. He fell to the ground immobile. Another member of the color guard grasped the flag and the Zouaves pressed on against the Confederate breastworks. By the conclusion of the action, the 146th had lost a total of 312 men killed, wounded or captured. Southern soldiers secured Williams as a prisoner and brought him into their own lines. He was soon paroled, and on June 14, 1864, was admitted to the Third Division Hospital in Alexandria, VA.

Williams was again allowed to return to New York to recover from his injuries. While at home, his term expired and on July 13, 1864, he mustered out of service and took up the role of war correspondent for the *New York Times*. In the fall of 1864, he covered the campaign of General Philip Sheridan's Federal troops in the Shenandoah Valley. While Williams was in Washington, D.C., President Lincoln asked him to recount the details of the victory at Winchester in September, which he did to the President's delight. As he prepared to leave, Lincoln "ordered" him to call again when he returned from the front. Williams assumed the President's invitation to be a mere pleasantry. However, a month later, after the battle of Cedar Creek, Williams was again in Washington and was greeted by the President's secretary, John Hay: "Mr. Lincoln saw you on the Avenue today. He is surprised that you have not come to see him." Williams rushed to the White House.

Lincoln greeted the young reporter commenting, "I am always seeking information and you newspaper men are often behind the scenes at the front [and] I am frequently able to get ideas from you which no one else can give." Lincoln listened to several escapades the correspondent had, then broke in: "What do you think of General Sheridan as an army commander?" Williams gave his favorable opinion. Then Lincoln reflected: "General Grant does seem to be able to pick out the right man for the right place at the right time. He is like that trip hammer I saw the other day . . . always certain in his movements, and always the same."

Not long after the meeting with Lincoln, Williams went to Petersburg to cover the grueling siege of the rebel city. General Grant read an article written by Williams for the *Times* concerning Sheridan's campaign in the Valley and enjoyed it so much that he invited the reporter to supper. When Richmond fell, Williams and many other reporters converged on the Confederate capital to record the scene. Williams returned to the Spottswood Hotel and inquired after his trunk that was left there four years earlier. The clerk informed him that it had been dismantled for use in the construction of artillery wheels.

Williams managed to get away from the field long enough to marry Marie Sophia Van Brunt on March 29, 1865. In 1867, he traveled to Mexico where he served both as a correspondent and as an aide on the staff of President Juarez. He also witnessed the execution of Emperor Maximilian at Queretaro. In 1868, he was appointed Brigadier General and Chief of Artillery in the Army of Guatemala and later served in the Peruvian Army. From 1870-73 he worked as the managing editor of the *New York Times,* and from 1875-76, he was the managing editor of the *New York Herald.* Later, he acted as the night editor of the New York *World* and the *Recorder.*

In 1884, Williams completed his novel *Bullet and Shell,* which remains popular today. He also edited the *Memorial War Book.* He fathered three daughters. By 1915, all of his daughters had died and he and his wife resided in West New Brighton on Staten Island. In November 1920, his wife passed away. The next month, Williams fell ill with pneumonia and died on December 31, 1920, at the Staten Island Hospital. He is buried at the Green-Wood Cemetery in Brooklyn.

George Forrester Williams lived life to the fullest. On one occasion, Williams and another reporter whisked the Prince of Wales away from his Fifth Avenue Hotel to a local bar to introduce him to a mint julep while the royal escort fretted over his disappearance. Even several Civil War wounds could not diminish Williams' spirit. From the poor orphan boy, he developed his talents as a soldier and a writer. With this unique combination, Williams provided precious glimpses of the common Civil War soldier in the field that have been cherished by past generations and will remain so in the future.

The Century Magazine
Vol. XXVIII -- October, 1884 -- No. 6

LIGHTS AND SHADOWS OF ARMY LIFE

It is a gratifying fact that the actors on both sides of the great American Civil War have been prolific in their contributions to our war literature, for the time will come when these personal recollections will be of priceless value. To those having no personal knowledge of the vicissitudes and fascinations of military service, its perils, privations, and pleasures, it may seem strange that the veterans who served in the Federal and Confederate armies should so fondly recall incidents in their campaign; and this propensity is often made the subject of jest among those who never saw a charge or felt a wound. But when a man has spent a week in toilsome marches toward battle, and then faced the enemy when death was hovering in the air, it is not easy for him to forget the fatigue, the hunger and thirst, the blanket-bed by the roadside, the hot skirmish on the picket-line, the gallop of the battery into position, the steady advance in line of battle, or the fierce charge at a turning-point in the engagement. Though these scenes make but little impression on his mind at the moment, they all come back to him in after years, and he is surprised to find how clearly he can recall each little incident. It is this faculty that leads the veteran, whether he wore the blue or the gray, to talk lovingly of the days when he carried the musket or the sword. Only men who have served under Grant or Lee, Sherman or Hood, Hooker or Longstreet, Meade or Jackson, Sheridan or Stuart, Thomas or Johnston, can realize how deeply the memory of the tremendous struggle has been impressed on the minds of the participators.

When the reverberations of the guns in Charleston harbor roused the people of the two sections to a realizing sense of the situation, they knew so little about war that none anticipated that the struggle would occupy more than a few months. With this false idea of the tenacity and courage of their antagonists, both Federals and Confederates entered the field with an amount of impedimenta that was truly laughable. Regiments had more camp equipage in 1861 than sufficed for a brigade

9

or a division in later years. Handsome tents, capable of accommodating a dozen men, made picturesque camps, with their fluttering pennons and painted tops. Mess chests, heavier than a caisson box, were considered essential to the proper comfort of a company's officers, though some of them lived to see the day when not even a colonel indulged in such a luxury. Young men, fresh from the domestic hearth, were furnished with more clothing and blankets than a mule could carry; consequently the wagon trains in the early days of the war presented formidable obstacles to successful prosecution of campaigns. Northern and Southern soldiers were alike in their fondness for hunting-knives and revolvers, while a pair of boots reaching to the knee was often provided for prospective marches. It is a well-known fact that many Confederate volunteers brought negro servants with them, though it was soon discovered that these sable attendants were only useful in consuming provisions needed for the fighting-men in the ranks. On both sides a love of finery and picturesque uniforms was manifested, but when rain and mud had spoiled this finery, soldiers found greater comfort in clothing of a more sober and enduring description. On the Federal side some half dozen Zouave regiments retained their wide, flowing breeches and tasseled fez, but the various German, French, and Italian costumes disappeared after the first campaign, when the opposing armies settled down to the tremendous struggle before them. There were stern lessons to be learned by the soldiers on both sides of the sectional line, before they were ready to become trained veterans; but with experience came patience under fatigue and privation, and coolness when called to face danger and death.

One of the hardest lessons for the American soldier was the necessity for military discipline and etiquette. It seemed odd to the youth who carried a musket that he must not be on familiar terms with an old schoolmate because the latter wore gold lace on his shoulder or collar. Many a young man, fresh from college, found himself subject to the arbitrary orders of his father's clerk; and the stern, inflexible rule of military life was so foreign to republican customs, it was difficult at first to teach the rank and file how necessary was discipline and unquestioning obedience. When regiments were formed at the outbreak of the war, officers on both sides were selected by ballot, the consequence being that many incompetent men were given command, and it was not until the troops had been in the field for some months that this condition of affairs was changed.

Laughable incidents of the lack of respect shown to officers in those early days might be related. When General Magruder was marching down the Peninsula at the head of a Confederate column, he halted at a farmhouse and ordered dinner. Entering the room where it had been served, he was amazed and indignant at finding one of his soldiers seated at the well-spread table, devouring the viands intended for himself.

"Sir!" thundered the general, as he drew his handsome figure up to its full height, "sir, do you know whose dinner you are eating?"

"No, I don't," replied the intruder, carelessly, as he refilled his plate, "And what's more, I don't care, so long as the victuals are clean."

General Magruder saw the point and retreated in good order, leaving the soldier to enjoy himself to his full content.

A Federal colonel, noticing that the sentinel in front of his tent omitted the usual salute due to his rank, called him to account.

"See here, Colonel," replied the soldier, "what good does it do you to have me present arms every durned time you take a notion to cross my beat? Aint you kinder putting on airs?"

It was often necessary to speak sharply to some laggard in the ranks while at drill, and, on one occasion, an officer had to pay special attention to one in his company with whom he had been on terms of social intimacy when there was no thought of war in the land. Finally, exasperated by what he deemed to be a deliberate attempt to mortify him, the soldier shouted out:

"Tom Wyncote, just you wait until we break ranks, and I'll give you one of the greatest lickings you ever got in your life."

A few months later, Captain Tom would have sent his friend to the guard-house. As it was, he laughed with the rest of the company, and explained that he had intended to exercise no special tyranny. The offender against military etiquette saw his error, and, being ashamed of himself, paid stricter attention to duty, and rose to high rank before the close of the war.

A Confederate private in the Louisiana Guards was sharply reprimanded by his superior officer, whose social rank he deemed beneath his own.

"It's all very well for you, George Weatherly, to talk to me that way now," he exclaimed wrathfully; "you wouldn't dare to do it if we were in New Orleans without that lace on your cuff."

The officer was brave enough, for, forgetting his position, he pulled off his coat, saying: "There, Frank Peyton, I don't wear lace on my shirt-sleeves. Come on!"

The two men were just beginning to spar at each other, when their cooler comrades separated them and pointed out the folly of the proceeding.

The time soon came, however, when the men who carried the musket were as great sticklers for military etiquette as their officers, resenting any neglect on the part of the latter in returning salutes. In some regiments the discipline was so strict that the men on post as sentinels were on the alert to discover any delinquency of their superiors. At Federal Hill, Baltimore, Colonel (afterward General) Warren gave orders to his Zouave guards that only officers in uniform were to be admitted into camp. One bright Sunday morning in August, 1861, General Dix, who commanded the troops guarding the city, walked over from Fort McHenry attired in an old linen duster, instead of the brass-buttoned and velvet-cuffed coat belonging to his rank. Attempting to pass the line of sentries, in company with an aide, the old general was amused at finding a musket barring his passage, while the aide, with his glittering shoulder-straps, was permitted to enter.

"Why do you stop me, my man?" inquired the general, quietly.

"My orders are only to admit officers in uniform," was the reply.

"But don't you see that this is General Dix?" exclaimed the aide, angrily.

"Well, between you and me, Major," said the Zouave, his eyes twinkling with amusement, "I see very well who it is, but if General Dix wants to get into this camp he had better go back and put on his uniform."

"You are quite right, sentry," remarked the general. "I'll go back and get my coat."

An hour afterward the general, in full uniform, approached the camp, and, allowing the guard reserve to be called out, accepted the salute due his rank and position, and the incident increased his admiration for the entire command.

At Yorktown the same Zouave regiment performed guard duty at the head-quarters of the commanding general. One day, as a test, General McClellan, while bareheaded and without uniform coat, passed and repassed the sentinel near his tent, only to find that the soldier paid no heed to his presence. Demanding why the customary salute was not given, he was informed that the sentries in the regiment did not salute a general or any other officer who happened to be in his shirt-sleeves. The reply delighted General McClellan and gained promotion for the educated soldier.

Camp life afforded many pleasures. The mails being regular, news from loved ones at home delighted the hearts of the way-worn and battle-scarred veterans. Company cooks were in their glory among their pans and kettles, the cry "Fall in for soup" sounding merrily in the ears of men tired of munching dry hard-tack or frying soaked biscuits in melted pork fat. The coffee was more abundant in quantity and better in quality, so the soldier's stomach was satisfied. Camp amusements had but little variety, but they were thoroughly enjoyed. Reading was a passion with most men, and books went the rounds until they were worn out by constant use. Newspapers were always plentiful, the army newsboys being a decided feature at the front. No sooner did an army halt within reach of these enterprising fellows than they were to be seen galloping from brigade to brigade distributing daily papers to eager buyers. Searching first for the dispatches relating the movements of his own command, the soldier turned next to learn tidings from other sections. With what delight the veterans read descriptions of actions they had taken part in, and woe to the unfortunate correspondent who chanced to make a blunder; he received no mercy from these stern and intelligent critics. Army newsboys were always ready to face danger while endeavoring to carry their bundles of papers into the lines. A bright young fellow started one morning from Harper's Ferry to join the troops assembling in the Shenandoah Valley under Sheridan. He had scarcely descended from the heights at the back of the town, when he found himself closely pursued by a party of Mosby's guerrillas. Mile after mile he galloped over the hard, macadamized road toward Charlestown, clinging to his bundles of papers and hearing a bullet whistle by his ears now and again as he proceeded. He finally escaped capture by the fleetness of his horse, but the soldiers were puzzled by finding the papers full of holes where the Confederate bullets had left their marks. Such adventures were, however, so common that neither soldier nor newsboy thought much about them. Newspapers formed a bond of fellowship between Eastern and Western armies, for from the daily journals they gleaned the news of each other's movements. The intelligence that Sherman's troops had reached the sea-coast came one evening to the Army of the Potomac in the columns of a Washington journal, and as the newsboys galloped along the lines of entrenchments before Petersburg they were followed by tumultuous cheers, until it seemed as it the whole army was uttering one mighty shout of gladness. The Confederate pickets, hearing the cheers, were anxious to ascertain the cause, and, when informed, a deep silence fell on Lee's lines. There was scarcely any musketry that night, and not a single piece of artillery disturbed the slumbers of the opposing armies. The sale of newspapers was an enormous source of profit, and so keen became the competition, the Government was compelled to dispose of the privilege to the highest bidder. At one time the sum of seventy-five thousand dollars per annum was paid for the exclusive right to sell newspapers in the Army of the Potomac, the money being devoted to the benefit of the hospitals.

NEWSPAPERS IN CAMP

Going into winter quarters was to the veteran what holiday time is to the school-boy. First of all there was the feeling that you were settled down for a time, the prospect of a long and much-needed rest, with an increase of personal comfort. The dreary boxes of hard bread were exchanged for broad sheets of fresh loaves from the Government bakeries. The sutler and the paymaster arrived, and every table groaned with simple but high-priced luxuries. Hut-building grew into an art. A few men of mechanical instincts would explore the woods in search of all sorts of odd-shaped roots and branches, creating out of these unpromising materials specimens of rustic work remarkable for neatness in design. Usually huts were built of rough logs, split in half to give the interior walls a finish. Shelter tents were stretched over rafters, the chinks between the logs were stopped with wet clay, and a chimney completed the edifice. Six men formed a mess, shelf-like bunks affording sleeping space at either end. In the center stood a cracker-board table, with a few stools or a couple of chairs made out of flour barrels. The muskets and equipments hung on pegs on either side of the door, which was made of canvas on a frame, or the universal resource, a cracker-box. In these snug huts the men forgot their trials and privations, and enjoyed the simple pleasures at their command. Chess, checker, and backgammon boards were obtained from the sutler or manufactured, and it was a poor hut that could not boast of a pack of well-thumbed cards. These games served to relieve the tedium of winter life, for in stormy weather there was not much drilling and very little fatigue duty. A great deal of pipe-carving was done, the roots of laurel being abundant, while the ambitious devoted their leisure to

WINTER CAMP

15

inventing patent machines. One of the most valuable agricultural implements now in the market owes its origin to a soldier mechanic, who completed the details in a winter hut.

Musicians were a great feature of winter camp-life. It mattered little what the instrument was as long as it made music. Violins, flutes, banjos, and the sonorous accordeon [sic] were to be found in every regiment. Round the instrumentalist clustered the vocalists, *al fresco* concerts being frequently given in the presence of appreciative audiences and huge, roaring fires. And these performers were ambitious in their efforts. I once heard the Anvil Chorus sung in fair Italian to the accompaniment of an orchestra that only boasted one bit of brass, a battered cornet. There were plenty of drums, and a neighboring battery furnished the anvil and sledges. Sometimes a shade of sadness would be cast over the rough assemblage as some favorite song would recall a noted singer who during the previous summer had found a soldier's grave on the battlefield. When books were scarce, readers would be appointed to read a volume of Bulwer, or Scott, or Dickens, the hut being full on such occasions. The rule about extinguishing lights at taps was seldom enforced while in the winter quarters, and many a pleasant hour was passed in listening to the voice of a good reader.

HOME, SWEET HOME (THE CIGAR-BOX VIOLIN)

Outdoor sports were not overlooked, being encouraged by thoughtful officers for the healthful exercise they afforded. Snow-ball battles were frequent, and it sometimes happened that whole brigades had a merry fight with these missiles; the strategy displayed was often of a high order, showing how well the soldiers were studying their trade. As a rule gambling was forbidden; the vice, indeed, was seldom indulged in, for men preferred sending their slender and hard-earned pay to those at home, instead of wasting it at cards. Letter-writing was a daily occupation, and the outgoing mails were always heavy. Home was the central thought, the longing to return there unconquerable, a stern feeling of duty alone keeping the armies together.

Some men were constantly engaged in beautifying their temporary dwellings, inventing new conveniences each succeeding day. Others were noticeable for the care they took of their arms and equipments, constantly polishing buttons and belt-plates, or burnishing gun-barrel and bayonet. A few practiced the manual of arms, or diligently studied military tactics as laid down in the school of the battalion and brigade. It often happened that in a brigade movement an incorrect order would be given, the offending field-officer discovering his error by the murmurs of discontent among his men. Waggish colonels frequently pretended to make mistakes, but the soldiers were quick to detect them, and refused to obey the order. But there were men who could not appreciate the necessity for drill or the comfort of neatness. They were ready enough for battle or picket, and would fight with coolness when on the field; yet, while keeping their weapons in good working order and seeing that their ammunition was dry, they saw no need for further effort. This class was never content unless they were on active service, and gladly volunteered to take the place of some ailing comrade for picket, preferring the excitement of the outposts to the humdrum life in regimental camp, with its dull routine of drill and fatigue details.

Picket life was always enjoyable, especially in the early spring-time, then signs of a approaching campaign multiplied. The warm air, filled with fragrance by the budding trees and forest flowers, was an agreeable change, the sentinels along the exterior lines being alert and watchful. As the season advanced frequent exchanges of coffee and tobacco were made by the pickets. A stump midway between the opposing lines usually marked the place of meeting, and it was curious to watch Federals and Confederates gravely sitting round a rubber blanket amicably bartering their wares. A tea-cupful of ground coffee was the equivalent for a plug of tobacco, and when coffee failed hardtack formed a convenient substitute. These soldiers seldom gave information about the armies, the subject being ignored; but the men eagerly compared notes about previous battles and campaigns, and were always delighted to meet Confederates belonging to commands they had fought against.

"What brigade do you belong to?" would be asked.

"Mahone's."

"Why, it was you fellows we charged on at Chancellorsville."

"Yes. And didn't we give it to you hot, though."

"Ah, that was because we could not use our artillery. You fellows fought well that day."

"So did you. It was a mighty hard fight while it lasted. How many cups of coffee have you got there?"

Thus did these American soldiers pay willing tribute to each other's prowess. Had the work of reconstruction been left to the fighting-men of the North and South, much of the bitterness of that period would have been avoided.

To the true soldier picket duty was a positive pleasure. The knowledge that in his hands rested the safety of the army made the most thoughtless grave. Slowly pacing his beat the sentinel listened to every sound, watched every movement. A scampering squirrel among the dead leaves, a twittering bird in the branches over his head, the robin hopping over the grass,--all were noticed in silence; but let a movement occur in the opposing line, and every musket was instantly cocked, while warning words ran rapidly along the chain of posts. A chance shot by some excited sentinel gaining an angry response, the whole line would soon be ablaze. Bullets whistled through the trees as the musketry grew in strength, and considerable ammunition would be wasted before orders came to stop firing. When the advance began, and the pickets received instructions to move forward and engage the enemy, every man ran to the line and work opened merrily. Night duty was naturally the most trying, for then there was the danger of surprise; but when the soldier was relieved he rolled himself in his blanket and slept calmly, knowing that his comrades were watching over him in their turn.

The long marches incident to campaigns were very trying, even to the artillery and cavalry, who had horses to assist in carrying their burdens. For the infantry a march meant an amount of fatigue only appreciated by those that have endured it. Compelled to rely upon himself for the transportation of food and extra clothing, the Federal soldier maintained a pace, though he frequently carried ten days' rations, a canteen of water, a twelve-pound musket, and eighty rounds of ball-cartridge. To this were added a piece of shelter tent and a change of under-clothing. Twenty miles was an ordinary day's work, but it often happened that the corps was compelled to cover twice that distance. The Antietam and Gettysburg campaigns were notable for the long and painful marches performed by both Federal and Confederate columns, though the latter found them less difficult, as they carried fewer supplies. Once on the move, an army never heeded the weather. Tramping over roads ankle-deep in dust, and under a burning sun, the men toiled uncomplainingly, their throats parched with thirst and their faces bathed in sweat. In rain that drenched them to the skin they splashed through mud in open country, clambered over mountain passes or trod the meadow-grass out of sight. Pushing through villages, fording streams, clattering over bridges, on they pressed, anxious and eager to meet the foe. Foot-sore and weary after a forced march, it only needed a sharp roll of musketry in front, or the boom of artillery on the flanks, to stiffen every muscle and gather up the laggards. In a moment the line was ready for battle. When the bugles sounded the halt, how gladly the veterans built fires, erected shelters, and prepared supper. The pickets told off, the main body slumbered as only tired soldiers can sleep. Most men took a pride in holding their places in the ranks, but a rapid movement naturally threw out the foot-sore and ailing, who limped painfully after their more fortunate comrades, in company with the incorrigible and persistent straggler. Men who in time of peace could not be induced to exert themselves when ill or in pain, would on a campaign persist in dragging their blistered and swollen feet over the rough ground in hopes of being able to get forward in time for the threatening engagement. This class of men entertained for the habitual straggler a detestation they were not slow to express, though it had very little effect upon the vagabonds who thus lingered at the heels of the army. A few of these confirmed stragglers were brave enough when a battle began, and usually managed to reach their command as it went into action; but the majority were simply skulkers, for who very little

19

mercy or consideration was shown by the untiring and remorseless provost-guards as they came up sweeping before them all the human debris behind the army. When a soldier became a confirmed straggler, the habit seemed incurable; and no sooner did a corps get fairly on the move that these idle fellows disappeared. They haunted farm-houses in search of food, and too often for useless plunder, rendering themselves a nuisance and a terror to the inhabitants. While endeavoring to escape from the irksome movement in column, the straggler frequently did twice as much tramping as the more orderly troops accomplished.

"Coffee-coolers," as these stragglers were commonly called, from their habit of bivouacking in convenient fence corners and nooks among the trees, were possessed by that vagabondish instinct which impels so many men to become tramps in the present day. Lazy and impatient of control, the confirmed coffee-cooler was irreclaimable. In camp he performed his military duty in a perfunctory and unwilling manner, the fear of punishment alone keeping him from open rebellion. Too cowardly to desert in the field, he hung on the skirts of the army while it was on the march, shirking the picket-line and the battle-field, thus leaving the better men the task of meeting the enemy. Coffee-cooling, as a habit, grew upon a man as does the love of intoxicating liquor, and once it fastened itself upon him, the coffee-cooler, like the drunkard, was beyond all hope. They were jolly fellows, however, in their way, these coffee-coolers, ever fond of a song or a good story with which to while away the time. One song had as many verses to it as there were regiments in the field. A single stanza will suffice to show the real object of coffee-cooling:

"Boil coffee on a rail
Over a fire in the gale --
    Ain't I glad to get out of the regiment!"

This was the sole aspiration of the straggling, wandering, idle vagabond,--to get out of the regiment. That accomplished, he was in his element, and lived a sort of gypsy life until driven by hunger or the provost-guard back to duty.

In the rear of a column were also to be found the head-quarter wagons and pack-mules. Loaded with officers' baggage, and supplies to their full strength, theses mules plodded patiently beside their attendants, while occasionally a field-piece with disabled team labored painfully over the road, sadly out of place. In the distance ahead glistened the muskets of the troops in line, with frequent glimpses of silken banner or pennon, as they fluttered in the faint breeze. In front it was all martial pomp and glory, in the rear clusters of hobbling men or wearied animals, while beside them sauntered a score or two of idle scamps, loitering beyond the reach of military discipline. Hark! There booms a cannon, and the sharp rattle of musketry follows. In an instant the scene changes. The foot-sore forget their blisters, the sick their weakness, and all hurry forward. The mules begin bellowing as they are led into the fields, and the provost-guards drive up the stragglers. More cannon give tongue, the rolling musketry grows heavier and stronger, showing that warm work has already begun. The road is suddenly empty and silent, the army gains fresh strength, and the battle progresses furiously.

In the Western armies the bummer was a peculiar feature. Sherman skillfully used this class, for they foraged for the main body while it made its great march to the sea. Mounted on nondescript, hammer-headed horses, their muskets slung carelessly over their rude saddles, these bummers scoured the country for supplies, and it must be admitted that they did not disdain to search for hidden riches. These men seemed to discover buried property by instinct, and many a Southern housewife was agonized at seeing her silver spoons and tea-pot dug out of the garden beds before her door. Reckless of danger, these Western bummers carried terror and dismay wherever they appeared, though they sometimes paid dearly for their temerity, a short shrift and a rope over the nearest branch being their fate when captured.

The question has been often asked, "How do soldiers feel when in battle?" and it is one difficult to answer. A long experience among veterans in the ranks leads the writer to believe that the emotion experienced in going under fire is much the same with all men. To the raw recruit the crash of small arms and the roar of cannon were simply appalling; he felt that he was going forward to certain death. With pale cheeks and clenched teeth he held his place, determined to do his duty as best he might. If very much excited, he loaded his musket, and, forgetting to put on the necessary percussion-cap, went through the motion of firing, only to ram a fresh cartridge on top of the first one, when, for the first time using a cap, he was incontinently knocked down

21

by the tremendous recoil of his gun, and believed he was badly wounded. Instances are known where muskets have been found on battle-fields containing six or seven cartridges. Finally the green soldier discovers that he is not hurt, and that everybody does not get killed in an engagement, so he regains confidence and passes successfully through his baptism of fire.

To the veteran it is far different. He knows too well that every battle reduces the average chance of his escape, yet so habituated has he become to rattling fusillades and desperate charges, he scarcely heeds the danger surrounding him. The shriek of the shells over his head, the buzz of the bullets past his ear, are now familiar sounds; and trusting to the chances of war, the infantryman fires rapidly with his musket, or the artilleryman calmly rams home another charge of grape and canister as his battery opens at close range on an advancing body of the enemy. All men are naturally afraid of death, but the trained and experienced soldier learns to keep down that fear, and nonchalantly do whatever is required of him.

Many humorous incidents occurred on battle-fields. A Confederate colonel ran ahead of his regiment at Malvern Hill, and discovering that the men were not following him as closely as he wished, he uttered a fierce oath and exclaimed:

"Come on! Do you want to live forever?"

The appeal was irresistible, and many a poor fellow who had laughed at the colonel's queer exhortation laid down his life soon after.

A shell struck the wheel of a Federal field-piece toward the close of the engagement at Fair Oaks, and shivering the spokes, dismantled the cannon.

"Well, isn't it lucky that didn't happen before we used up all our ammunition," remarked one of the artillerists as he crawled from beneath the gun.

When General Pope was falling back before Lee's advance in the Virginia Valley, his own soldiers thought his bulletins and orders somewhat strained in their rhetoric. At one of the numerous running engagements that marked that disastrous campaign, a private in one of the Western regiments was mortally wounded by a shell. Seeing the man's condition, a chaplain knelt beside him, and opening his Bible at random read about Samson's slaughter of the Philistines with the jaw-bone of an ass. He had not quite finished when, as the story runs, the

22

poor fellow interrupted the reading by saying:

"Hold on, Chaplain. Don't deceive a dying man. Isn't the name of John Pope signed to that?"

A column of troops was pushing forward over the long and winding road in Thoroughfare Gap to head off Lee after his retreat across the Potomac at the close of the Gettysburg campaign. Suddenly the signal-officer who accompanied the general in command discovered that some of his men, posted on a high hill in the rear, were reporting the presence of a considerable body of Confederate troops on top of the bluffs to the right. A halt was at once sounded, and the leading brigade ordered forward to uncover the enemy's position. The regiments were soon scrambling up the steep incline, officers and men gallantly racing to see who could reach the crest first. A young lieutenant and some half dozen men gained the advance, but at the end of what they deemed a perilous climb, they were thrown into convulsions of laughter at discovering that what the signal men took for Confederate troops were only a tolerably large flock of sheep. As the leaders in this forlorn hope rolled on the grass in a paroxysm of merriment, they laughed all the louder at seeing the pale but determined faces of their comrades, who, of course, came up fully expecting a desperate hand-to-hand struggle.

It is perhaps needless to add that the brigade supped on mutton that evening.

As the army was crossing South Mountain the day before the battle of Antietam, General McClellan rode along the side of the moving column. Overtaking a favorite Zouave regiment, he exclaimed with his natural *bonhomie*:

"Well, and how is the Old Fifth this evening?"

"First-rate, General," replied one of the Zouaves. "But we'd be better off if we weren't living so much on supposition."

"Supposition?" said the general in a puzzled tone. "What do you mean by that?"

"It's easily explained, sir. You see we expected to get our rations yesterday, but as we didn't, we're living on the supposition that we did."

"Ah, I understand: you shall have your rations, Zou Zous, to-night," replied the general, putting spurs to his horse to escape the cheers of the regiment. And he kept his promise.

It was after the Antietam campaign that President Lincoln visited the army and made a running sort of review, each regiment standing to arms at its own camp to receive him. This same Zouave regiment had suffered terribly, and the President spoke to General McClellan about the slender appearance of the battalion.

"Oh, the Zou Zous are all right," remarked the general, "They can whip the devil round a stump any time."

"It would be a very small stump, then," replied the President, "or the devil would soon get away from them."

A THIRSTY CROWD

Toward the close of the siege of Petersburg a very large number of the men composing General Finnegan's Florida brigade deserted from Lee's lines. The fact became so noticeable that the Federal pickets took it up, and used to shout across the line:

"Say, Johnny, send General Finnegan over here. We want him badly."

"What for?" innocently inquired a Confederate soldier one day, on hearing the absurd request for the first time.

"What for? Why, to take command of his brigade, to be sure. It's nearly all over here now."

Every general of prominence had a nickname bestowed upon him by his troops. Some of these names were of a sarcastic nature, but usually they indicated the confidence of the men in their leaders of their admiration for them. General Grant was commonly known over the watch-fires in the Army of the Potomac as "Old United States," from

24

the initials of his name, but sometimes he was called "Old Three Stars," that number indicating his rank as lieutenant-general. McClellan was endeared to his army as "Little Mac." Meade, who wore spectacles, was delighted to learn that the soldiers had named him "Four-eyed George," for he knew it was not intended as a reproach. Burnside, the colonel of the First Rhode Island regiment, rose to the dignity of "Rhody" when he became a general. Hooker never liked the sobriquet of "Fighting Joe," though he always lived up to it during his career in the field. Pope was saddled with the title of "Saddle-bag John," in memory of his famous order about head-quarters being on horseback. His men used to say that their head-quarters moved pretty rapidly at times. Sigel, the German general, was known in the other corps as "Dutchy." Hancock won the brevet of "Superb," from a remark made by General Meade at Gettysburg, when the Second Corps repulsed Longstreet's men. Humphrey, being a distinguished engineer, was invariable styled "Old Mathematics." The Pennsylvania Reserves used to call Crawford "Physics," he being a surgeon at the beginning of his military career. Logan, with his long black hair and dark complexion, was "Black Jack" with his men. Sheridan, the cavalry leader, was "Little Phil," and Sherman's troops spoke of him as "Old Tecumseh." The sterling nature and steadfast purpose of Thomas earned for him the significant and familiar name of "Old Reliable." Alexander McDowell McCook, like Hooker, was called "'Fighting' McCook." The New York City regiments in the Fifth Corps changed Sykes to "Syksey." Halleck was derisively nicknamed "Old Brains," and Rosecrans had his name shorted to "Rosey." Lew Wallace was "Louisa" to the soldiers under his command; he was a great favorite for his fighting qualities, and the soldiers adopted that inappropriate name for want of a better. Kearney, who had left an arm in Mexico, was invariably known in the ranks as "One-armed Phil." Butler was styled "Cockeye," for obvious reasons. Kilpatrick was nicknamed "Kill," while Custer was called "Ringlets," on account of his long, flowing curls; and so the catalogue might be prolonged indefinitely.

Among the Confederates family nicknames were not so common as with the Federals. The soldiers of the Army of Northern Virginia usually spoke of General Lee as "Bob Lee." Little Mahone was best known as "Skin and Bone." Early was called "Bad Old Man," and Jackson will live in history as "Stonewall."

General George B. McClellan (left) was affectionately called "Little Mac" by his men in the Army of the Potomac. General Robert E. Lee was fondly known to the soldiers of the Army of Northern Virginia as "Bob Lee" or "Marse Robert." [Photos: Patrick A. Schroeder Collection]

With very few exceptions, the Federal generals commanding armies, corps, or divisions were favorites with their men. There were degrees, however, in the enthusiasm displayed by the soldiers for their leaders. McClellan was the idol of his troops so long as he remained in the field, and even to this day many a middle-aged man feels his heart grow warm when "Little Mac's" name is mentioned. General McClellan possessed that personal magnetism which distinguished Napoleon; and had his nature been as cold-blooded as that of the Corsican, there can be no question that McClellan would have been the most successful general on the Federal side. His face was a peculiarly engaging one, and when he galloped along the line of a corps, his cap lifted high in the air in acknowledgment of the salutes of his men, every soldier in the ranks seemed to feel that the general had recognized him individually. He was constantly looking after the comfort of his troops, and many anecdotes could be related of his checking his horse to secure

26

attention for some wounded or foot-sore soldier. The objects of his pity never forgot the incident, and as they multiplied during a campaign the men's admiration and enthusiasm increased. The day he was finally relieved from the command of the Army of the Potomac was a sorrowful one for the veterans of the Peninsular and Antietam campaigns, and he left the field regretted by every officer and man in the ranks.

Grant, silent and grave, seldom awoke enthusiasm among his soldiers, although they entertained from him a sincere regard and high respect; for they learned in time that this taciturn man, who rode over battle-grounds without a sword, chewing an unlighted cigar in his powerful jaws, was a true leader, and indeed, a great soldier. Knowing Grant to be resolute and tenacious, the rank and file fought under his command with steadiness and courage, appreciating the fact that every blow they struck would be followed by others equally strong and efficacious. Though the hero of Vicksburg and Appomattox seldom noticed the salutes of his men, it was evident that he appreciated them, and in these days of peace no general is more fond of recalling the good feeling that existed between him and war-worn veterans he led so often to victory.

Sherman was a good deal like McClellan in his anxiety for the welfare of the soldiers under him, and he was very happy in the manner of receiving their salutations. Nervous by nature, he was impetuous and easily angered, but under his faded and threadbare uniform beat a warm and tender heart. Recognizing the pregnant fact that war is necessarily cruel, he never hesitated to push his men forward in the face of a withering fire, but he was always ready on occasion to accompany the advancing line, being then cool and collected, though his face would be all aglow with the excitement of the moment. The Western armies loved "Old Tecumseh," and no man is more heartily welcomed at the annual reunions nowadays than General Sherman.

Thomas resembled Grant in his intercourse with his men, being steady and sedate, but a most vigorous fighter. He hated scenes, but under his calm exterior the knowledge that the troopers liked and respected him made his heart glad. When he first heard that his men had given him the sobriquet of "Old Reliable," his features relaxed, and a pleasant, gratified smile showed that he appreciated the compliment at its true value.

Meade was a great favorite, whether at the head of a division, corps, or the Army of the Potomac. Soldierly in his attire, he always appeared to advantage when mounted, and his graceful way of acknowledging the greetings of his men sometimes rendered them tumultuous. No general on the Federal side equaled him in wording bulletins. McClellan had a dashing Napoleonic style that was very captivating, but Meade adopted a far different method, for he took the troops into his confidence; told them that he relied more on their bravery and steadiness than his own generalship; asked them to do their best, and victory was certain. There is no question that the field of Gettysburg was won because every man who carried a musket had been told by his general that it was the soldiers' battle. That Meade was a favorite is shown by the nickname he was given by the army.

Sheridan was a *beau sabreur*, and managed to win the confidence and love of his troops. Passionate to the extreme, this brilliant soldier was sometimes harsh and often rude to his officers, but to the men in the ranks, collectively, he was always indulgent, though a strict disciplinarian.

Burnside was beloved by the Old Ninth Corps, but the disastrous result of his single battle while commander of the Army of the Potomac was fatal, and he failed to win more than respect from the whole body.

Hancock was the darling of the Old Second Corps, and a great favorite with the entire army. Those who have seen only the recent portraits of Hancock can have no proper conception of his appearance in the field. Spare in frame, and looking tall in the saddle, his tanned face was set off by a heavy mustache and goatee. Since the war "Winfield" has grown handsomer with his gray hair and shaven face, but in many a humble home throughout the land the old war photograph of the Second Corps leader is cherished by the veteran of that famous corps. Courteous in manner, dignified in appearance, and prompt in action, he was always successful, being followed by his men with a devotion seldom paralleled in the annals of the war.

Sedgwick much resembled Thomas in his intercourse with the soldiers serving under him, and the love of his men was shown by their erecting, at West Point, a splendid statue to his memory. Warren-- nervous and excitable--never so well satisfied as when moving up under fire--was, nevertheless, careful of his men, and was proud to know that they sometimes spoke of him as "Gouv." Logan, with his dark face and coal-black hair, could always move forward on the field, feeling sure that his men would follow with confidence and fight desperately. Kilpatrick and Custer were never so happy as when on a raid. Moving swiftly, they gloried in striking the enemy and carrying confusion into their ranks. Both were idolized by their men, and for the same reasons-- a total disregard of personal safety. Charging at the head of the column, these gallant cavalry leaders exulted in the excitement of the hour and the desperate nature of the movement. Custer's heroic death at the battle of the Big Horn is a signal proof of his headlong courage and the willingness of his men to follow him to the bitter end, under the most discouraging circumstances.

The impudence of American soldiers was very noticeable. One day, as General McClellan was riding through the camps at Yorktown, he was greeted with the salutation of "How are you, Ge--orge?" The general laughed at the incident and probably soon forgot it. But imagine a German soldier addressing Von Moltke in such fashion.

Army teamsters were never appreciated at their true value by soldiers in the field, for it was the general opinion that "any fool could drive mules." Those who tried the experiment found that the teamster's office was not a sinecure. The successful handling of six stubborn, pugnacious brutes, as army mules invariably were, required a degree of patience and an amount of skill and will-power only to be developed by long experience. When the roads were dry and even, wagon-driving was a pastime, but when the trains reached mountain passes, or the roads became seas of mud after heavy rains, then the task was indeed no joke. Mud, three feet deep, as tenacious as stiff clay could make it, rendered the movement of wagons and artillery a most difficult operation. The wheels were solid disks, the spokes and felloes being entirely hidden by the mass of mud they carried, and the labor for both men and animals was multiplied four-fold. Then the genius of the teamster was manifested. With a strange inexhaustible vocabulary of oaths at his command, and armed with a formidable snake whip, the driver used both with startling and telling effect. The air, blue with shocking profanity, and the huge whip whistling cruelly as it descended on the backs of the quivering brutes, gave them new strength, and the mired vehicle soon emerged from its muddy bed. It was a leading article of faith among teamsters that mules could only be driven by constant cursing, and they lived up to that belief with rare constancy.

Strange as it may seem, it is nevertheless a fact, that whenever an attempt was made to drive a team of mules without indulgence in profanity it invariably proved a failure, because the animals had become so accustomed to that method of persuasion they would not move without it. Teamsters, as a class, were brave and untiring, rendering important service in their peculiar sphere of duty, but they got very little credit for it from the rank and file, being generally looked upon as men who were unwilling to fight. That they could fight, however, was often proved, for the teamsters frequently saved their trains from capture by their stubborn resistance when attacked. Every wagon carried a loaded musket and the weapons were often used with deadly effect.

Many a brave mule driver died like a hero in defending the property intrusted to his charge, though there was seldom any record of such bravery.

To see an ordnance train gallop up on the battle-field was an exhilarating sight, for then the teamsters were in their glory. Coming up on the trot the wagons would be wheeled into line as cleverly as if the men were moving field-pieces into position, and the mules appeared to enjoy the occasion as much as their drivers, for they strained every muscle and obeyed every command with remarkable docility.

Contrabands, as the negro refugees were called, were constantly coming into the Federal lines. Sometimes on foot, laden down with a miscellaneous collection of household goods of very little value to any one except the owner, the patient contraband would confidingly approach the pickets, taking it for granted that he would be welcome. Simple in nature, the negro would walk quietly up the road, and seeing the sentinel, salute him respectfully with "Howdy, massa?"

"What do you want?"

"Ise come in, sah; Ise wants to be contraban'."

"And what will you do after you come in?"

"I dunno, massa. Ise willin' to do 'most anyting."

That was it. He was willing to do anything so long as he gained that precious boon, his personal liberty.

Sometimes a whole family would apply for admission, the grandfather, the women, and the children, seated in one of those nondescript vehicles to be seen only in the South. The wagon was frequently drawn by a miserable, half-starved mule and a cow, the ill-assorted animals pulling together in friendly but strange fashion. As

30

soon as the word was given to pass on, the whole group invariably broke out with a joyful hymn celebrating their entrance into the promised land.

Cavalry duty was the most agreeable and exciting branch of the service, for the mounted soldier was always in the van of the army on a campaign, or hovering on the flanks when the enemy threatened an attack. Moving swiftly from point to point, these men passed through a dozen hard skirmishes in a single day. Now swooping down on a train and destroying it on the spot, now seizing the entrance to a mountain pass or fighting for its possession, now dashing across rivers and driving in the stubborn pickets to enable the engineers to lay a pontoon bridge, the cavalryman always found plenty of hot work cut our for him. And when the enemy was retreating, how tenaciously did the tireless cavalry hang on his rear, cutting off stragglers, capturing pieces of artillery, and sometimes charging on the rear guard. Picturesque in their movements, reckless in courage, and always ready for a brush, the cavalry was the admiration of the infantry and the envy of the artillery. The foot soldier wished he had a horse to carry him and his equipments, and the gunner wished he could move about more rapidly. The cavalry leaders were all dashing, impetuous men, and with old soldiers the names of Sheridan, Pleasanton, Kilpatrick, Averill, Dahlgren, Custer, Stoneman, Merritt, Wilson, Hampton, Stuart, Imboden, and Morgan were the synonyms for bravery and desperate gallantry.

On the field of battle the American cavalry seldom made their appearance. At Gettysburg, Pleasanton and Kilpatrick made a swoop on Lee's right at the close of that desperate struggle, and the entire corps fought at Brandy Station at the beginning of that campaign. In the Shenandoah Valley the cavalry did a wonderful amount of field service. Released by the siege of Petersburg, Sheridan carried his troopers to the Valley, and in every engagement used the cavalry at a critical point to swing round on Early's flanks and throw them into confusion. The cavalry charge at the battle of Winchester must be ranked as one of the most brilliant episodes of the war.

Mention has been made of the humorous incidents happening on battle-fields, but there was very little fun to be found in the ranks when the army was arrayed in line of battle. Then everybody was serious. Orders were given in a quiet tone and obeyed with celerity and in perfect silence. Here the private was of more importance than his officer, for on his courage and coolness rested the issue of the struggle. If the men in the ranks stood fast and used their weapons with proper effect, a victory would be won; if they failed to hold their ground, all was lost. The officers could only direct what should be done; the men were to execute it. Then there was the feeling among both officers and men that in the presence of the enemy they stood on one common plane as to danger. The bullets flying over their heads and the shells screaming and shrieking in mid-air paid no heed to rank. Brigadiers and colonels, captains and lieutenants, were no better here than the humblest private. One of the most trying positions for a soldier is the movement of a line during a battle. The men have probably been fighting hard all the morning, only to find the fire of the enemy gradually slackening and finally ceasing altogether. Skirmishers are thrown out and word comes that the opposing line has fallen back.

THE HALT OF THE LINE OF BATTLE

Then orders are issued to move forward in line. Slowly, steadily, the several brigades step out, following their skirmish line over the fields,

32

through woods, and across ravines and ditches, until at length the men catch a glimpse of the enemy's line where it has taken up advantageous ground. "Halt" comes ringing down the line, and as the men obey and drop the heels of their muskets on the soft earth, they peer curiously at their adversaries, knowing too well that the next minute will probably bring them into mortal combat. Silent and thoughtful, the soldiers lean on their rifles, their faces blackened with powder, or bleeding from some slight wound a veteran never heeds. They feel no great desire to go forward, but are perfectly ready and willing to do so if their general so decides. Each man in the long line knows that if an advance is made some of them will not see the sun set, and he cannot shake off the feeling that perhaps his turn has come to join the silent majority. Look down the line, and you will see many a face, which has been the life and soul of the camp, now serious enough, for, as the veteran gazes at the corpses scattered over the field, he realizes the awfulness of the occasion. Suddenly the bugles utter their shrill notes and the silent line moves forward. Batteries behind them open fire, and under cover of these shells the advance continues. Then, as they come within musket range, the enemy greets the advancing body with a blinding volley of musketry, and men fall dead and wounded in every direction, the survivors coolly closing up the ranks and leaving them behind, as the next moment they make a rush to seize the position. The musketry grows hotter and hotter, the cannonading fiercer and fiercer, until suddenly a ringing cheer rises above the roar and racket, telling that the movement has proved successful and the enemy are once more in retreat.

Instances of personal heroism were frequent in both Federal and Confederate armies. One of the commonest of these was the rescue of wounded comrades under fire, and it was a proof of the generosity of the combatants that, whenever such efforts were recognized, the musketry would slacken and both lines join in cheering the rescuers. Scarcely a battle occurred without a dozen or more of these attempts, most of them begin successful, though it often happened that, instead of helping their comrades, the brave fellows ran to meet death, or like them to be stretched on the earth in an agony of pain. Such were some of the lights and shadows of army life on American battle-fields.

George F. Williams

CROSSING THE LINES

GEORGE F. WILLIAMS

On the morning of May 3, 1864, Grant set his columns in motion for what is now known in the history of the Civil War as the Overland Campaign. Heavy reinforcements had been coming in during February and March, the heavy artillery, in charge of the Washington defenses, being summarily torn from the long lines of forts lying between Centreville and Alexandria. Finally, the old 9th Corps, under General Burnside, came up along the line of the Rappahannock Railroad. Hitherto the new levies had arrived by train, and we knew that the advent of Burnside's men on foot was the near forerunner of a campaign that all realized would be a desperate and bloody one.

I had known General Burnside in Washington before the war, so spoke to him as he halted the head of his corps at Warrenton Junction, the camp of the regular division, under Ayres, lying close at hand.

"So, general," said I, "you've come back to join the old army once more?"

"Yes, and right glad am I to be among you fellows of the Army of the Potomac. All these woods and fields we have passed since leaving Alexandria seem so familiar to me. I suppose you regulars are ready for a move?"

"Yes, we have been in good trim for a month. Nobody knew you were coming, though, until news was brought by the trains that the 9th Corps was on the march hither. I imagine we shall not have to wait much longer, now that you have arrived."

"No; my orders were to make good time, and reach the Rapidan River by next Thursday. This is only Monday, so we have three more days' march to reach our destination. What's the news?"

"There have been some changes. Sykes has gone to the West, and Warren now commands the 5th Corps, while there are a lot of consolidations to make room for these tremendous regiments of heavy artillery. At first we thought they were brigades, as compared to our own commands."

"They will not be so big a few weeks hence," replied the general, with a grim smile. "From what I understand of Grant's plans, the

34

fighting, when once we get at it, will be terrible."

"That's what we all think," said I. "The new lieutenant-general is so silent, yet so earnest in his preparations, it portends some hard knocks. Do you know he hasn't issued a bulletin yet?"

"And he won't," said Burnside.

Then the general was surrounded by other army friends, who kept him busy answering questions, until it was time for the long column to move on. The following day orders came for us to leave our comfortable winter huts and advance towards the Rapidan. A few days after we crossed the river at Germanna Ford.

While I was on picket duty the afternoon before the general advance of the army, General Warren examined our line, and told me that the corps would cross the following morning.

Williams spoke with General Ambrose "Rhody" Burnside (left) commander of the Federal IX Corps and V Corps commander General Gouverneur "Gouv" Warren (right) before the Battle of the Wilderness. [Photos: Patrick A. Schroeder Collection]

"Do you think Lee will dispute our passage?" I asked, as the general mounted.

"No; he's too good a tactician for that," replied Warren. "Ordinarily it would be good strategy to oppose us on the bank of this river, but it would require too long a line, and result in a series of small battles, instead of a general engagement. You must remember that we shall enter a territory like that of Chancellorsville, a dense forest, where artillery will not be of much use. I fancy Lee will try to repeat his Chancellorsville tactics. Our defeat, with the river in our rear, would be a crushing one."

"Why do you talk of defeat?" said I. "Surely you don't class Grant with Hooker?"

"Of course not. You may make up your mind that once across the river, you will never see his side again, unless you should be wounded."

The general rode away, while I flung myself beside my bivouac fire, to ruminate on coming events. I was lost in revery, when a sergeant came up from the ford.

"They're signaling down below, sir," said he.

"Who are?"

"The Southern pickets. They want coffee and bread for tobacco."

"Do any of our men want to exchange?"

"Yes, sir; Lieutenant Murray sent me to ask if you will allow them."

"I suppose so. Matters have been so peaceful along the line, there can be no harm," I replied, rising with the intention of visiting the ford.

On descending the road, I found Lieutenant Murray waiting for an answer to his message; a dozen of the men having gathered a few loaves of soft bread and a haversack nearly full of coffee and sugar.

"So our friends on the other side want to trade," said I, with a laugh.

"Yes," replied Murray, "this bread will all spoil, while there tobacco will not. What do you say captain?"

"Oh, go ahead; but be quick about it, men."

Waving a not very clean white handkerchief tied to a ramrod, three or four of the men sprang into the icy water of the narrow river, and the exchange was rapidly made. While the barter was going on, I noticed an officer standing on the opposite side of the bank, watching the proceeding, his new gray uniform revealing a manly figure.

"I wonder what his uniform cost him," said Lieutenant Murray, on perceiving what I was looking at.

36

"A thousand dollars, probably, in their paper money. You know our own greenback dollars are worth only fifty cents in gold."

"No wonder the poor fellows are so shabby," said Murray.

"It's not the coat that makes the soldier, Murray," I replied. "You and I have often been shabby enough after a campaign."

"But then we could always get a new outfit on reaching permanent camp."

"True; all the more reason for respecting these men in gray. They are fighting against terrible odds."

THE EXCHANGE WAS RAPIDLY MADE

As I spoke, the Confederate officer lifted his hat and shouted across the river:--

"Thanks, gentlemen, for your courtesy. I wanted the bread and coffee for a brother officer who is ill."

"We are pleased to help you," shouted the lieutenant, as the Southerner bowed and withdrew with his party.

Soon after daylight the following morning, our corps came up, bag and baggage, to cross the ford, and we pickets resumed our places in the line. It was not until late in the afternoon that the entire corps got across, being delayed in order to give way to a division of cavalry that had been sent to feel the ground we were to occupy. That night we slept on our arms, undisturbed by the rattle of the picket musketry that was blindly waged in the darkness.

Comrades of Williams in the 146th New York Zouaves. Corporal Conrad Neuschler (left) was the third man in the regiment to carry the colors at the Battle of the Wilderness. Corporal Edwin Glover (right), like Williams, was among those captured in the engagement. The 146th lost 312 men killed, wounded, and captured during their charge. [Photos: Patrick A. Schroeder Collection]

Breakfast over, we waited for orders to move forward, but it was after ten o'clock before a movement was made, and then it was only for the purpose of clearing the ground for some other corps to cross. Another day passed, but I comprehended that Grant was forming his line of battle, for we could see that the 2d and 6th Corps were taking position on our left.

About eleven o'clock on the morning of May 5th, orders came to go forward in line. Crushing through the dense undergrowth that so choked the woods, we went along quite merrily, though very few faces escaped a scratch or two from the brushwood. Suddenly our brigade came to an opening, interspersed with young pines. Scarcely had our first line emerged from the woods, when a volley of musketry met us.

On moved the line, however, every step being marked by the falling of dead and wounded men. The volleys now grew more incessant and vengeful, yet I could not distinguish the opposing line, except by the blaze of the muskets. So far we had not been able to fire a shot, and as I remembered that we had been ordered to go forward and "feel the enemy," I realized we were doing so with a vengeance.

Looking up, I saw that the supporting lines were coming along in good style. When we reached the edge of the woods, and saw the Confederate breastworks, a rolling cloud of white smoke was rising steadily from it, the blaze of the muskets making great flashes of light. Instinctively halting, our men began returning the fire, but it was of little avail, because of the strong position occupied by our opponents. Then a couple of field pieces opened briskly from a rise in the Gordonsville turnpike, the shells crashing through the trees, over our heads. But the gunners had advanced too close to the Confederate infantry line, and had to retire before the fierce volleys poured on their guns. Meanwhile, the musketry on both sides grew hotter and hotter, on our being increased by the arrival of the second line.

"Colonel Jenkins has been killed," said the sergeant-major, as he passed along the rear. "Where's the lieutenant-colonel?"

"Down on the left," I replied, "if he hasn't been hit."

Suddenly a bugle sounded, and our line began to fall back in a stubborn sort of way, and the next instant I felt a hot, stinging pain shoot through my thigh, and I fell. A moment after I was left behind, and lost consciousness. How long I remained in that state I know not, but when I recovered my senses, the battle on that part of the field

Commanders of the 146th New York Volunteer Infantry at the Battle of the Wilderness, May 5, 1864. Colonel David T. Jenkins (left) and Lieutenant Colonel Henry H. Curran (right) were both killed while charging Confederate breastworks at Saunders' Field. [Photos: Patrick A. Schroeder Collection]

seemed to be over. Wondering if I had strength left to crawl back, I was about to make the attempt, when four of five Confederate soldiers passed me.

"I saay, sargint," exclaimed one of the men, "this officer isn't so dead after all. Shall we carry him to the ra'ar?"

"Might as well," replied the sergeant.

Two of the men lifted me in their arms, and swiftly carried me off the field. I was still so faint from loss of blood I did not care much what became of me. I saw that we passed through the main line of the Confederate army, and a few minutes after my bearers laid me down beside a small brook; one of them, taking my cap and dipping it into the stream, gave me a delicious drink.

No further attention was paid to me, apparently, and I was beginning to wonder why I had been made a prisoner, when more wounded officers and men were brought, both Confederate and Federal. Then a surgeon came and examined friend and foe alike, as we lay in a row in

40

the narrow wood-road. When my turn came, the surgeon shook his head, saying, in a low tone:--

"No use doing anything for him. His thigh blade is split. He cannot live very long."

"You are mistaken, doctor," I replied; "I will live yet to fight you fellows again."

"Shouldn't be surprised if you did," remarked the surgeon. "Men who talk like you do, are not easily killed."

"Why do you think my thigh blade is split?" I persisted.

"Oh, I see it's a bullet I felt," replied the surgeon re-examining my wound. "You may as well send him to the rear."

When I had been slung in a blanket, I noticed several other Federal officers being treated in the same manner. We were all carried over the road for a mile or two, until we reached Robertson's Tavern. There I and my fellow prisoners were deposited under the locust trees that bordered the road.

The afternoon was by this time tolerably well spent, the shadows of the trees lengthened, and the air grew colder. My wound was becoming stiff and painful, while a few of my companions were moaning. That the Confederate army was changing position was evident by the passage of a long column of infantry across the fields, while several batteries rumbled along the road that crossed the Gordonsville pike at right angles. Rolling musketry could be distinguished on the Confederate right, punctuated by frequent discharges of artillery. Lying on the tender grass, I listened to these sounds and watched the movements of the troops with curious ear and eye, but I felt no very great interest in the scene, in my helpless condition. Then a strong body of cavalry passed, followed by more infantry.

"I wonder what is going on in front," said a young, boyish officer who lay near me.

"Pretty hard to tell," I replied, "except that the fighting is nearly over for to-day."

"I suppose they'll begin it all over again to-morrow," said the young fellow, after easing his pain with another groan.

"Of course. You might know that."

"How I wish we were not prisoners!"

"No use wishing that. We *are* prisoners, so must make the best of it."

A Confederate battery, evidently belonging to reserve artillery, now came slowly up the road, and halted near us. The men, seeing the group of Federal wounded, gathered round us. Suddenly, they stepped back to make way for three or four mounted officers.

The one in front drew rein, and, bending over his saddle, asked me, in a measured, penetrating voice:--

"Is General Grant in command of your army, sir?"

"No, sir," I replied, "General Meade commands the army, but the lieutenant-general is with us."

"It amounts to the same thing," said the officer, in a musing tone. "Tell me, sir, how many men had you when you crossed the Rapidan?"

"Excuse me, sir," I retorted, rather ungraciously. "Though I am wounded and a prisoner in your hands, you cannot expect me to give you any information regarding the Federal forces."

"You are quite right, sir. I beg your pardon."

Then he put spurs to his steed and galloped away, followed closely by the others.

"What officer was that?" I asked, as the artillerymen again approached us.

"That was General Robert E. Lee," responded a sergeant. "He commands the hull of the Army of North Varginny." Then, at a signal, the battery moved away, and we were again alone.

While wondering at the chance that had brought me face to face with the great Confederate leader, I looked about me to see if there were any guards, but could see none. It was evident that we were considered too helpless to attempt an escape. The shades of evening deepened into night, and my pain was deadened by increasing coldness of the atmosphere. Finally, I fell into an uneasy slumber, only to be awakened by the noise of horses' hoofs.

Looking up I saw a small force of cavalry, which began picketing their horses near a barn. Soon a few fires were lighted, and at the nearest one stood a group of officers. A groan from the lips of one of my companions attracted their attention, and one of them walked over.

"Are you wounded, sir?" said he to me, in a sympathetic tone.

"Yes."

"And are you hungry?" he continued.

"A little."

"Is General Grant in command of your army, sir?"

Going back to his fire, the officer stooped, and then quickly returned.

"Here's a nice hot pone of corn-bread, sir," said he, placing it in my hands the fragrant-smelling food. "I was so kindly treated in your hospitals while myself a wounded prisoner, I always try to help a Federal officer whom I find in the same fix."

"Thank you, sir," I replied, munching the pone, which tasted delicious. "This is almost as good as our soft white bread we had in winter quarters."

"I got some of your bread two or three days ago down at one of the fords," said he. "One of my comrades was ill."

"That was at Germmanna Ford, wasn't it?" I asked.

"You are right," he exclaimed. "How did you know?"

"It was my picket post."

"Indeed! I am very glad to have met you, sir," said the officer. "But I am sorry you are a prisoner."

"It cannot be helped now, though I wish your men had not carried me off the field."

By this time the other officers had drawn near, and the coincidence of our meeting was explained. Finding that nothing had been done for us in the confusion, they ordered a huge fire built, a little off the road, and we were all placed comfortably around it. A few blankets were also procured, and some food for those who cared for it. Then a sentry or two was set over the horses, and both Federals and Confederates fell asleep on their common mother earth.

On awakening the next morning, just after daylight, I found that the cavalry had departed. I never saw my Confederate friend again, neither did I ever learn his name. Pain kept me awake until the hospital corps came and made better arrangements for our comfort. I remained there for nearly three weeks, when I was fortunate enough to be able to make my escape to Alexandria.

But I have never forgotten my experience while crossing the lines between the Army of the Potomac and the Army of Northern Virginia, after the Battle of the Wilderness. Thus it was that the men who fought in the front learned to respect each other, and the incidents I have related were of more frequent occurrence than would be imagined by those who never heard the buzz of a bullet or the shriek of a shell during a fierce engagement.